DARE
TO EXCEL

GBEMINIYI EBODA

DAЯE
TO EXCEL

DARE TO EXCEL

Copyright 2006 by Gbeminiyi Eboda
ISBN 9783774212

Published and printed in Nigeria by
MOVE YOUR WORLD INT'L.
P.O. Box 21089, U.I. Ibadan, Nigeria.

First Print 2004
Second Print 2009
Third Print 2015

CONTENTS

1. Success *p2*

2. Uniqueness And Discovery *p24*

3. Friendship *p52*

4. Order *p62*

5. Maturity *p70*

6. Discipline *p78*

7. Diligence *p82*

8. Forgiveness *p92*

9. Courage *p98*

Final Words *p104*

SUCCESS

> **❝** *Success is no respecter of location, fertility is not in the LAND, but in the Mind. Whatever your mind cannot COMPREHEND, your life cannot APPREHEND.* **❞**

———•———

And theLord said unto Abraham...lift up now thine eyes and look from the place where thou art...For all the land which thou SEEST, to thee will I give it.
Gen 13:14-15

———•———

❝ Jesus did not just come to show man God, but also to show man man. The only thing a man cannot do is what he has not attempted to do. If he will DARE it, he will do it. **❞**

———•———

If thou canst believe, all things are possible to him that believeth.
Mark 9:23

———•———

" The Spirit
of WORK is the
spirit of
WORTH. **"**

---•---

*Seest thou a man diligent in his
business...he shall stand before.
kings.
Prov 22:29*

---•---

❝ To keep
GOING is to
keep
GLOWING. **❞**

---•---

*Go ye into all the world, and
preach the gospel to every.
creature.
Mark 16:15*

---•---

❝ The zenith of an accomplishment is the genesis of another one. This may be your bus-stop, but definitely not your end-stop. Keep on keeping on. **❞**

---•---

...Reaching forth unto those things which are before.
Phil 3:13

---•---

**“ Inventions
are simply intentions
that enjoyed
attention. ”**

———•———

*Give thyself wholly to them that
thy profiting may appear to all.
1 Tim 4:15*

———•———

❝ Real success is
progressive. To succeed
you must aspire to
exceed all that
currently exists. **❞**

———◆———

*But the path of the just (is) as the
shining light, that shineth more
and more unto the perfect day.
Prov 4:18*

———◆———

❝ Success is not
hereditary. Failure is
not genetic. It is all a
function of
choice. **❞**

―――●―――

*I have set before you life and
death, blessing and cursing,
therefore choose life.
Deut 30:19*

―――●―――

10

**❝ Success
is relative to progress.
It is making
measurable progress in
a reasonable amount of
time. ❞**

———•———

*To everything there is a season,
and a time to every purpose
under the heaven.
Eccl 3:1*

———•———

❝ Success
begins at the point
when a man can no
longer tolerate failure.
Remember that
whatever you can
tolerate, you cannot
alleviate. **❞**

———•———

*By your sword you shall live, And
you shall serve your brother; And
it shall come to pass, when you
become restless, That you shall
break his yoke from your neck.
Gen 27:40 NKJV*

———•———

❝ A man that
is blessed by God
cannot be less with
men. **❞**

———•———

*...and God talked with him,
saying, As for me, behold, my
covenant (is) with thee, and thou
shall be a father of many nations.
Gen 17:3-4*

———•———

❝ There is a price
to pay for greatness.
There is an inevitable
process to success. The
more intense the
process, the more
immense the
proceeds. ❞

---•---

*The refining pot (is) for silver and
the furnace for gold, but the LORD
trieth the hearts.
Prov 17:3*

---•---

**ᏪᏪ Success
begins at a point at
which your seed finally
finds its field. ᏮᏮ**

---

*Then Isaac sowed in that Land
and received in the same year an
hundredfold: and the Lord blessed
him.*
Gen 26:12

" You have been
sentenced to success.
No bail granted. **"**

———•———

*Before I formed thee in the belly I
knew thee and before thou comest
forth out of the womb I sanctified
thee, and I ordained thee a
prophet unto the nations. Jer 1:5*

———•———

ﾝ The worst
Epitaph reads thus
"Here Lies the Remains
of a Man that would
have been, should have
been, could have been,
but never
Became". ﾝﾝ

———•———

*Rachael died by me in the land of
Canaan in the way, when yet
there was but a little way to come
to Ephrath.*
Gen 48:7

———•———

" A dream empowers you not to mistake a bus stop for your end stop, not to compromise your real destination for a cheap imitation. **"**

———•———

It is pleasant to see dreams come true, but fools refuse to turn from evil to attain them.
Prov. 13:19 NLT

———•———

❝ Success is never over night, but overtime, though the reward may come overnight. **❞**

———•———

For in due season, we shall reap, if we faint not.
Gal 6:9

———•———

" The last of God's
creation is man. Every
other thing created
after man, was created
by man. **"**

———•———

*I have said, ye are gods. All of you
children of the Most High.
Psalm 82:6*

———•———

“ Success is an aggregate of inputs. ”

---•---

For whatsoever a man soweth
that shall he also reap.
Gal 6:7

---•---

❝ Inventions have not ended. Only seekers are few. **❞**

---•---

Seek, and ye shall find.
Matt 7:7

---•---

—●—

UNIQUENESS
AND DISCOVERY

—●—

" He who has not disconnected psychologically, emotionally and financially from parents cannot provide a covering for a woman. His roof will be leaking. "

---•---

Therefore shall a man LEAVE his father and mother...
Gen 2:24

---•---

❝ Honour
is the venison every
child owes his or her
parent. If you must live
long and live well, give
it fully. **❞**

---•---

Honour thy father and mother
which is the first commandment
with promise.
Eph 6:1-3

---•---

" Physiological
development and
financial adequacy do
not equate marital
competence. **"**

---•---

*And Judah saw there a daughter
of a certain cannanite ...and he
took her and went in unto her.
Gen 38:2*

---•---

❝ If a man is not seeking first the kingdom of God and you feel an affinity for him, then God is not the one adding you to him. It is the devil! **❞**

Do not be unequally yoked together with unbelievers. For what fellowship has righteousness with lawlessness? And what communion has light with darkness?
2 Cor 6:14 NKJV

❝ Marriage is supposed to be a haven, not an oven. it should be a heaven on earth experience. ❞

———●———

That your days may be multiplied ...as the days of heaven upon the earth.
Deut 11:21

———●———

“ Don't just
NOURISH a child,
NURTURE him. **”**

---•---

*Train up a child in the way he
should go and when he is old, he
will not depart from it.
Prov 22:6*

---•---

❝ Marriage
is for BLISS and not for
BLISTERS, but it must
be between two
wholes, not unequal
halves. **❞**

---•---

*Two are better than one for they
have a good reward for their
labour.*
Eccl 4:9

---•---

❝ More parents
now think it is
primitive to
correct/spank their
children. Not to correct
your child, is a
weakness on your part.
God will hold you
responsible for what
his tomorrow
becomes. **❞**

———•———

*Because his sons made themselves
vile and he restrained them not.
1 Sam 3:13*

———•———

❝ Not to read, is to become like a reed; unstable, easily shaken and without conviction. The reader is the Leader. ❞

---•---

Also that the soul be without knowledge, it is not good.
Prov 19:2a

---•---

> **❝** A man's status
> is not a function of his
> stature **❞**

---•---

*There be four things which are
little upon the earth, but they are
exceeding wise.*
Prov 30:24

---•---

" Humility is the
hallmark of all true
achievers. When you go
for a meeting,
leave the teacher in you
at home, take the
student along. **"**

---•---

*By humility and the fear of the
Lord are riches and honour and
life.*
Pro 22: 4

---•---

" There is a difference between growing old and growing up. Everybody is growing old, but only a few are growing up. **"**

---•---

And the child grew and waxed strong in spirit, and was in the deserts till the day of his shewing unto Israel.
Luke 1:80

---•---

> ❝ Failure
> is supposed to be a
> teacher, not a killer, a
> trial of your faith, not
> its burial. ❞

---•---

*That the trial of your faith, being
much more precious than of gold
that perisheth though it be tried
with fire, might be found unto
praise and honour and glory at
the appearing of Jesus Christ.*
1 Pet 1:17

---•---

“ Your past experience is not meant to imprison your future, but to improve it, not to deform your future, but to inform it, not to endanger your future, but to empower it. **”**

———•———

Remember ye not the former things, neither consider the things of old. Behold I will do a new thing; now it shall spring forth; shall ye not know it? I will even make a way in the wilderness and rivers in the desert.
Isa 43:18-19

———•———

" Accept your individuality and express your originality. If the whole world were to be just like someone, the world will be boring. **"**

---◆---

Having then gifts differing according to the grace that is given to us, let us use them.
Rom 12:6a NKJV

---◆---

❝ Knowledge
increases your value.
AGGREGATE it, so you
can APPRECIATE in
value. **❞**

———•———

*A man of knowledge increases
strength.
Prov 24:5.*

———•———

❝ Laziness will
generate lust in
anybody, keep the
fire burning!
Be fervent. **❞**

———•———

*Not slothful in business, fervent in
spirit, serving the Lord.
Rom 12:11*

———•———

" Human beings
call distractions side
attractions **"**

---•---

*And as thy servant was busy here
and there he was gone.
1Kings 20:40*

---•---

" Outside
diligence, life will yield
no meaningful
dividend. **"**

---•---

*He that tilleth his land shall be
satisfied with bread.*
Prov 12:11

---•---

❝ Ability
without responsibility
turns you into a
liability **❞**

---•---

*And he saw that rest was good
...and became a servant unto
tribute.*
Gen 49:15

---•---

❝ Your outlook
determines your
outcome. What you
expect, you
experience. **❞**

———•———

*...and that which I was afraid of is
come unto me.*
Job 3:25

———•———

45

❝ All things work together for good to them that have God as a partner in their labours. ❞

---•---

...and we know that all things work together for good to them that love God,to them who are the called according to his purpose.
Rom 8:28

---•---

❝ The day you
approach with great
expectation leaves you
with great experiences.
It is expectation that
causes a miracle to stop
at a man's
address. **❞**

---•---

*For surely there is an end, and
thine expectation shall not be cut
off.*
Prov 23:18

---•---

" The future
you cannot design is a
future you do not
deserve. "

---•---

*And the Lord answered me and
said, Write the Vision, and make it
plain upon tables, that he may
run that readeth it.*
*For as he thinketh in his heart, so
is he.*
Hab 2:2, Prov 23:7

---•---

❝ A dream
is a mental definition
of your desired
destination. If you
cannot define it, you
may never
find it. **❞**

———•———

*For behold, we were binding
sheaves in the field and lo, my
sheaf arose, and also stood
upright and behold your sheaves
stood round about and made
obeisance to my sheaf.*
Gen 37:7

———•———

❝ If you don't
know where you are
going, congrats! You are
already there. **❞**

———•———

*There is none greater in this
house than I; neither hath he kept
back any thing from me but thee,
because thou art his wife: how
then can I do this great
wickedness, and sin against God.
Gen 39: 9*

———•———

❝ You don't need ten keys to open a door, just the right one. You don't need to know everybody, just the right buddies. You don't need to know everything, just have the right knowledge. **❞**

———•———

And Jesus answered and said unto her, Martha, Martha, thou art careful and troubled about many things: But one thing is needful: and Mary hath chosen that good part, which shall not be taken away from her.
Luke 10:41-42

———•———

—•—

FRIENDSHIPS

—•—

" Inspiration grows or goes via association. **"**

———•———

Iron sharpeneth iron; so a man sharpeneth the countenance of his friends.
Prov 27:17

———•———

" If you give
him pre-eminence, he
will bring you to
prominence. **"**

———•———

*In all thy ways acknowledge him,
and he shall direct thy paths.
Prov 3:6*

———•———

66 There is no
way a man will walk
with giants, eat what
they eat and remain a
dwarf. **99**

———•———

*He that walketh with the wise
shall be wise.
Prov 13:20*

———•———

❝ Valley experiences are good at times. They reveal who your true friends are. At Golgotha, only Jesus' true aides were left. Even an enemy comes to your party. **❞**

Thou preparest a table before me, in the presence of mine enemies; thou anointest my head with oil, my cup runneth over.
Psalm 23:5

❝ Corporate achievement is God's brain child. No vision gets executed in isolation. Every journey embarked upon in isolation leads into desolation. **❞**

---◆---

And God said, LET US...
Gen 1:26

---◆---

❝ Friendship
is by choice not by
force. You were born
with a taste, be
selective. **❞**

———•———

*Can two walk together except
they be agreed.
Amos 3:3*

———•———

❝ It takes
righteous contacts to
keep having meaningful
impact. **❞**

---•---

*Iron sharpeneth iron; so a man
sharpeneth the countenance of
his friends.*
Prov 27:17

---•---

❝ Environment
has the greatest
influence on any living
thing. Therefore, man is
a true reflection of his
environment. **❞**

———•———

*Blessed is the man that walketh not in
the counsel of the ungodly, nor standeth
in the way of sinners, nor sitteth in the
seat of the scornful. But his delight is in
the law of the LORD; and in his law doth
he meditate day and night. And he shall
be like a tree planted by the rivers of
water...*
Psalm 1:1-3

———•———

" There are no age mates in life only Grace Mates. There are no classmates in life only light mates or what I call illumination colleagues. **"**

Thus Melzar took away the portion of their meat, and the wine that they should drink; and gave them pulse. As for these four children, God gave them knowledge and skill in all learning and wisdom: and Daniel had understanding in all visions and dreams.
Daniel 1:16-17

ORDER

❝ For your life to
be divorced from
routine and be married
to results, sentiments
must be discarded,
principles must be
embraced. **❞**

———•———

*The slothful man roasteth not
that which he took in hunting; but
the substance of a diligent man is
precious.*
Prov 12:27

———•———

❝ There is a difference between MOTION and PROGRESS. Order is a requisite for progress. Organise that you may not agonise. **❞**

Let all things be done decently and in order.
1 Cor 14:40

❝ Reason before routine, routine before results. Life is an accumulation of details. **❞**

———•———

Make thee an ark of gopher wood; rooms shalt thou make in the ark, and shalt pitch it within and without with pitch. And this is the fashion which thou shalt make it of... A window shalt thou make to the ark, and in a cubit shalt thou finish it above.
Gen 6:14-16

———•———

❝ If you must
walk the walk, you start
by talking the talk. It's
your statements that
determine your
placements. **❞**

---

*Death and Life are in the power of
the tongue: And they that love it
and shall eat the fruit thereof.
Prov 18:21*

❝ Only those
that live
successively, end
successfully. **❞**

---•---

*For precept must be upon
precept...line upon line...here a
little and there a little.
Is 28:10*

---•---

66 Mind your language. Those who complain never obtain. Those who grumble crumble. **99**

———•———

And when the people complained, it displeased the Lord; and the LORD heard it; and his anger was kindled: and the fire of the Lord burnt among them, and consumed them that were in the uttermost parts of the camp.
Num 11:1

———•———

———•———

MATURITY

———•———

" Significance
is being the best you
can be and being
blessed for being the
best. **"**

---•---

*So Job died, being old and full of
days.*
Job 42:17

---•---

❝ It takes
sincerity to discern
between good and evil,
but it takes maturity to
discern between good
and right. **❞**

---◆---

*All things are lawful...but all
things edify not.*
1Cor 10:23

---◆---

" Though
maturity is not a
function of age, yet it is
developed with
TIME. **""**

---•---

*And the child GREW and waxed
strong in the spirit...
Luke 1:80, 2:40, 52*

---•---

" Puberty is no liberty for flippancy. Abuse of puberty has increased the world's poverty. **"**

---◆---

This is the will of God...ABSTAIN from Fornication.
1Thess 4:3-4

---◆---

❝ Men of standards usually end up with stardom. ❞

———•———

*...but Daniel purposed in his heart
that he will not defile himself with
portion of the king's meat
Daniel 1:8*

———•———

" To abide is
to abound. **"**

---•---

*Those that be planted in the
house of the Lord, shall flourish in
the courts of our God.
Psalm 92:13*

---•---

———•———

DISCIPLINE

———•———

> ❝ Unction and
> Passion are
> independent variables.
> Holy oil cannot subdue
> youthful lust, only
> discipline
> will. ❞

———•———

*But I keep under my body and
bring it into subjection; lest that
by any means, when I have
preached to others, I myself
should be a castaway.*
1 Cor 9:27

———•———

“ What you
can't afford,
avoid, don't try to own
what will make you
owe; don't empty
the future into
the present. **”**

---•---

*Owe no man any thing, but to love
one another: for he that loveth
another hath fulfilled the law.*
Rom 13:8

---•---

—•—

DILIGENCE

—•—

❝ In life, there is the PRIZE though there are usually consolation prizes too. What is your choice, to be extolled or to be consoled? To be envied or to be pitied? ❞

———•———

And jabez called on the God of Israel saying, Oh that thou wouldest bless me indeed and enlarge my coast and thine hand might be with me, and that thou wouldest keep me from evil, that it may not grieve me! And God granted him that which he requested.
1 Chr 4:10

———•———

" Make yourself essential where you work. An essential staff is the last to be considered for retrenchment but the first to be recommended for promotion. Be a value adder! **"**

———◆———

Seeth thou a man diligent in his business? He shall stand before kings: he shall not stand before mean men.
Prov 22:29

———◆———

❝ While some
have chosen to make
caves out of clay,
others have chosen to
build castles
out of it. **❞**

---•---

He becometh poor that dealeth
with a slack hand: but the hand of
the diligent maketh rich.
Prov 10:4

---•---

❝ You were made for arrival. Don't give up on the eve of your coronation. Don't plant for another to reap. Stay on course and keep on keeping on! ❞

———•———

If thou faint in the day of adversity, thy strength is small.
Prov 24:10

———•———

**❝ The rewards
that diligence brings,
only diligence
can maintain. ❞**

———◆———

*...but the substance of a diligent
man is precious.
Prov 12:27*

———◆———

❝ Your position
in life is not a function
of your opposition but
of your
disposition. **❞**

———•———

And behold,there was a man named
Zacchaeus ...And he sought to see Jesus
who he was...And he ran before ,and
climbed up into a sycomore tree to see
him...And when jesus came to the Place
,he looked up and saw him and said unto
him, Zacchaeus...for today I must abide
at thy house.
Luke 19:2-5.

———•———

**❝ A day
without hay is a day
without pay. ❞**

---•---

*He who does not work let him not
eat.*
2Thess. 3: 10.

---•---

❝ Only the diligent will become the eminent. ❞

———•———

The hand of the diligent shall bear rule.
Prov 12: 24.

———•———

FORGIVENESS

**❝ Bitterness
is a defilement, it
defiles you, it defiles
others
around you. ❞**

———•———

*Looking diligently lest any man
fail of the grace of God. lest any
root of bitterness springing up
trouble you, and thereby many be
defiled.
Heb 12:15.*

———•———

**❝ To be bitter
doesn't make
life better. ❞**

———•———

*And Saul was very wroth...Saul
eyed David from that day
forward.
1 Sam 18:8-9.*

———•———

❝ The strongest voice in your life should not be from your past but of your Future. ❞

---•---

Brethren, I count not myself to have apprehended: but this one thing I do, forgetting those things which are behind, and reaching forth unto those things which are before.
Phil 3:13.

---•---

❝ The sin you retain, you repeat. The sin you retain, you reflect. The sin you retain makes you detained. **❞**

———•———

But if you do not forgive neither will your father which is in heaven forgive your trespasses. Mark 11:26.

———•———

** Great men are
not people that never
failed, rather they are
people that never gave
up. TRY again! **

———•———

*For a just man falleth seven times,
and riseth up again: but the
wicked shall fall into mischief.
Prov 24:16*

———•———

———●———

COURAGE

———●———

" It takes a heart
to make a mark. It takes
a will to win.
It takes guts to leave
the rut. **"**

---•---

*I have set the Lord always before
me, because he is at my right
hand, I shall not be moved.*
Psalm 16:8

---•---

" No one can
successfully
resist the person whom
God assists. **"**

---•---

*What shall we then say to these
things? If God be for us, who can
be against us?
Rom 8:31.*

---•---

" A problem
may be lasting, but it
cannot be everlasting,
Everlasting is the
exclusive preserve of
Almighty God. **"**

---•---

*For his anger endureth but a
moment; in his favour is life:
Weeping may endure for a night
but joy cometh in the morning.
Psalm 30:5*

---•---

❝ No mountain
can withstand your
Rock, because He is the
Rock of Ages. **❞**

———•———

*He only is my rock and my
salvation; he is my defence; I shall
not be greatly moved.
Psa 62:2*

———•———

❝ Never forget
that the things that are
higher than you are not
higher than The Most
High! **❞**

———•———

*The things which are impossible
with men are possible with God.
Luke 18:27*

———•———

——●——

FINAL WORDS

——●——

" Life can only be sustained through progress. A man that stops moving, will start mourning. If you will not move, you will soon be mourned. **"**

———•———

Arise ye, and depart for this is not your rest.
Micah 2:10

———•———

❝ Every man's elevation is due to God's visitation, which is a function of man's expectation. **❞**

---•---

And thy visitation hath preserved my spirit.
Job 12:10b

---•---

ff Never struggle
with a season you are
through with. Don't put
comma or a question
mark where God has
put a full stop. **]]**

———•———

*And the same day, when the even
was come, he saith unto them, Let
us pass over unto the other side.
Mark 4:35.*

———•———

❝ Wherever He is given preeminence, He brings to prominence. ❞

Those who honour me I will honour.
1Sam 2:30.

FIRST THINGS FIRST

Man was created with an instinct to worship, fellowship and dominate. You sure need God in your life. The greatest decision you can ever make is to accept the Lordship of Jesus into your life as this has an implication on your life here on earth and hereafter. Have you accepted Jesus into your life? Are you born again? If you are not sure, say these words:

"Lord Jesus, I believe you died on the cross, and was buried and rose again from death because of me. I come to you today. I am a sinner and cannot help myself. Forgive me my sins. Cleanse me with your blood. Today, I accept You as my Lord and Saviour. Thank you for saving me. Amen.

Dear friend, welcome to the family of God. Be free to be a part of God's people around you.

I will love to read from you.

E-mail: reveboda@gmail.com

Twitter: @niyieboda   Facebook: Gbeminiyi Eboda

OTHER BOOKS

BY

THE AUTHOR

BECOMING A MONEY MAGNET

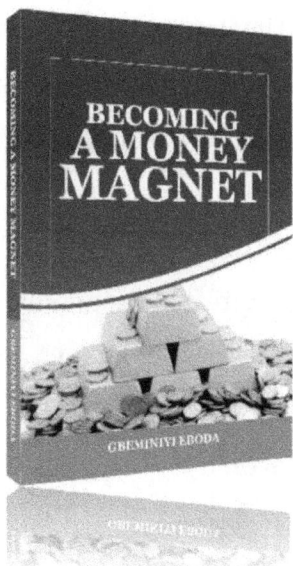

There's money everywhere! But it is only within the reach of those who will dare to reach out for it. A copy of this book will empower your mind with principles of financial intelligence.

SINGLE WITHOUT WRINKLES

A toast to every spinster, the truth for every bachelor. This book is God's wisdom delicately packaged for the lady to disentangle her from the web of influences and past experiences hindering her from being maximised.

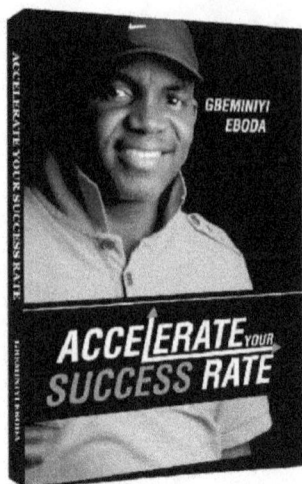

"The impossible is the untried". This book is suitable for individuals and organisations who will dare the odds and venture the impossible to become more and do more and ultimately have more.

This text is another archetypal to guide you from living a life of activity into a life of higher productivity!

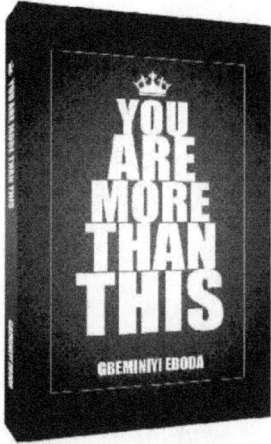

There's no barrier to success. It's all about you. This book will help you find a way out of ignorance and develop a very strong database that will usher you into the future that you have always dreamt of.

You are the main character in this book! This text is a blueprint or guide which if followed will take you from where you are to where you want and passionately desire to be in life and the whole concept is to help unearth the value on your inside from its potential form.

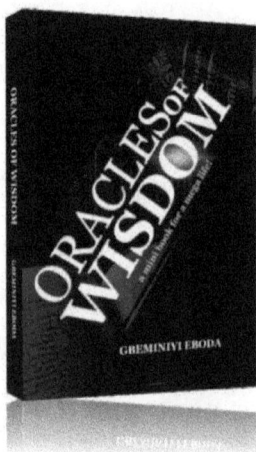

In this book are wisdom nuggets covering different aspects of life. It's a mini book for a mega life!